THE ANIMAL KINGDOM

Mammals

Bev Harvey

CHELSEA CLUBHOUSE

An Imprint of Chelsea House Publishers
A Haights Cross Communications Company
Philadelphia

Chelsea Clubhouse
1974 Sproul Road, Suite 400
Broomall, PA 19008-0914

The Chelsea House world wide web address is www.chelseahouse.com

Library of Congress Cataloging-in-Publication Data

Harvey, Bev.
  Mammals / by Bev Harvey.
  p. cm. — (The animal kingdom)
  Summary: A simple introduction to the characteristics of mammals in general and of select species.
  ISBN 0-7910-6981-8

  1. Mammals—Juvenile literature. [1. Mammals.] I. Title.
  QL706.2 .H37 2003
  599—dc21

                                                      2002000979

First published in 2002 by
MACMILLAN EDUCATION AUSTRALIA PTY LTD
627 Chapel Street, South Yarra, Australia, 3141

Copyright © Bev Harvey 2002
Copyright in photographs © individual photographers as credited

Edited by Angelique Campbell-Muir
Page layout by Domenic Lauricella

Printed in China

Acknowledgements
Cover photograph: African elephant, courtesy of Martyn Colbeck—Oxford Scientific Films/Auscape.

ANT Photo Library, pp. 4, 10, 11, 25, 28, 29; Klein/Hubert-Bios/Auscape, pp. 16, 19; Martyn Colbeck—Oxford Scientific Films/Auscape, pp. 1, 24 (top), 27; Jean-Paul Ferrero/Auscape, pp. 18, 21, 23; Ferrero-Labat/Auscape, p. 26; Jeff Foot/Auscape, p. 9; Brett Gregory/Auscape, p. 7 (bottom); M. P. Kahl/Auscape, p. 24 (bottom); David Parer & Elizabeth Parer-Cook/Auscape, p. 15; Alan Root/Survival Anglia—Oxford Scientific Films/Auscape, p. 12; Norbert Rosing—Oxford Scientific Films/Auscape, p. 13; Gerard Soury—Oxford Scientific Films/Auscape, p. 6 (bottom); Australian Picture Library/Corbis, p. 17; Coo-ee Picture Library, pp. 8, 14, 20; Getty Images, pp. 5, 6 (top & center), 7 (top); Photography Ebiz, p. 22; photolibrary.com, p. 7 (center).

While every care has been taken to trace and acknowledge copyright the publisher tenders their apologies for any accidental infringement where copyright has proved untraceable.

Contents

Mammals

Mammals are vertebrates. A vertebrate is an animal that has a backbone. Mammals are **warm-blooded** animals. They have hair on their bodies, and they feed milk to their young.

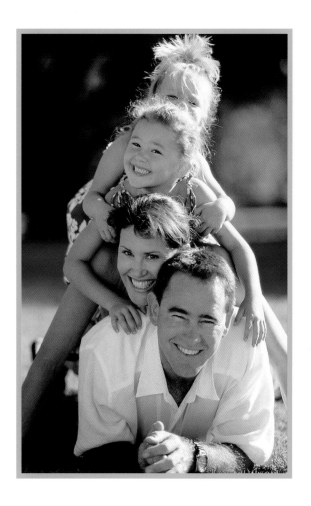

Some mammals live on land, and some live in the water. Bats are mammals that can fly. Mammals can be huge, like whales. They can be tiny, like mice. Humans are mammals too.

Types of Mammals

There are many types of mammals.

Humans are mammals.

Grizzly bears are mammals that live in North America.

Dolphins are mammals that live in the ocean.

Elephants are the largest
mammals that live on land.
They live in Africa and Asia.

Platypuses are mammals that
live in streams in Australia.

Cats are mammals. People
all over the world keep
cats as pets.

Features of Mammals

Milk

Female mammals have mammary glands for making milk. All mammals feed milk to their young after they are born. Young mammals drink milk to help them grow until they can find their own food.

Hair

All mammals have hair. Polar bears have thick hair to keep warm. Humans have more hair on their heads, but less hair on their bodies. Dolphins are born with a few whiskers on their noses. The whiskers fall out later.

Tails

Many mammals have tails or tailbones. Some monkeys use their tails to hang from trees.

Movement

Most mammals have four limbs. Limbs can be legs, arms, flippers, or wings. Different limbs help different mammals walk, run, swim, dive, fly, climb, jump, or glide.

This possum is gliding from one branch to another.

Eating Habits

Most mammals are herbivores. Herbivores eat only plants. Horses and cows are herbivores. Some mammals, such as the aardvark, are insectivores. They eat only insects.

This aardvark is eating termites inside a termite mound.

Other mammals are carnivores. Carnivores eat only meat. They hunt for their food. Lions are fast and powerful hunters. Humans are omnivores. Omnivores eat both plants and meat.

Young Mammals

Nearly all mammals have live births. The young mammal develops inside its mother's body. After birth, the young mammal still depends on its mother for food and protection. Female mammals usually raise their young alone.

This newborn echidna is drinking its mother's milk.

Platypuses and echidnas are the only mammals that lay eggs. They are called monotremes. After hatching, a young monotreme still drinks milk from its mother. Kangaroos belong to a group of mammals called marsupials. A newborn marsupial is very tiny. It clings to its mother. Some female marsupials have pouches to carry their young.

Domestic Cats

People all over the world keep cats as pets. Domestic cats developed from either African or Asian wildcats. All of the cat breeds we see today are related to each other.

Cats are mainly carnivores. Some people keep cats to kill pests such as mice and rats. Cats have sharp claws to catch and hold their **prey**. They use their sharp teeth to bite and eat.

A female cat will attract a male cat when she is ready to **mate**. After mating, the male leaves. The female will be **pregnant** for about 65 days. Females usually give birth to four kittens in one litter.

Kittens are born blind and helpless. They drink milk from their mother's body. After six weeks, kittens can eat on their own. They are ready to leave their mother.

Kangaroos

Kangaroos live in Australia. A kangaroo has powerful back legs with long feet. For short distances, it can hop at speeds up to 30 miles (48 kilometers) per hour. Its thick, long tail helps it balance while hopping.

Kangaroos can jump as far as 16 feet
(5 meters) in one leap. Kangaroos are very
strong. They will fight by hitting with their
front paws and kicking with their hind legs.

Kangaroos are herbivores. They eat grass and leaves. They live in woodlands and forests, but they can also survive in dry open plains. They rest during the day and come out to feed in the cool of the night.

Kangaroos are marsupials. A newborn kangaroo, or joey, crawls into its mother's pouch. Inside, it finds a **teat** on its mother's body and drinks milk.

As the joey grows, it starts to leave the pouch. It learns to find food on its own.

Elephants

There are two types of elephants. The African elephant is larger. It lives in the forests and deserts of Africa. The smaller Indian elephant lives in India and Southeast Asia.

An African elephant's ears reach its shoulders.

An Indian elephant's ears are much smaller.

Female elephants and their young live together in a herd. Adult males often live alone. A male will find a female to mate, but then he will leave. A female elephant is pregnant for about 22 months. After it is born, the calf drinks milk from its mother. Other females in the herd help care for the calf.

An elephant's trunk is really its upper lip and nose. An elephant uses its trunk to eat and drink. It picks up grass, roots, fruits, and leaves and places them in its mouth. It sucks water into its nostrils and then squirts the water into its mouth. An elephant also uses its trunk to make loud calls.

An elephant uses its trunk in many ways. It can pull down trees. It can pick up small objects so it can look closely at them. Elephant tusks are actually large teeth. An elephant uses its tusks for digging, taking bark off trees, and carrying large loads.

Endangered Orangutans

Orangutans are large apes that live in trees. They use their long arms to climb and swing through the branches. They rarely climb down to the ground. They sleep in the treetops every night.

Orangutans once lived in many tropical rain forests in Asia. Now they are found only on the islands of Sumatra and Borneo. Orangutans are **endangered** because people have been cutting down trees in the rain forests. New laws protect orangutans and their rain forests.

29

Animal Classification

The animal kingdom is divided into two main groups of animals: invertebrates and vertebrates. In this book, you have read about mammals.

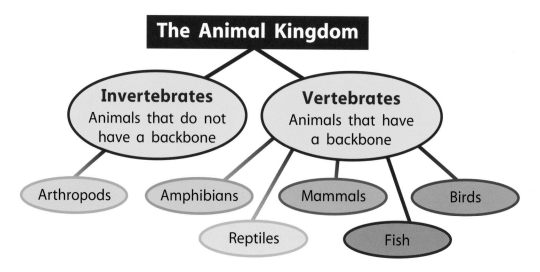

Question   What have you learned about mammals?

Answer   Mammals:
- are vertebrates
- are warm-blooded
- drink their mothers' milk
- have hair.

Glossary

endangered   a type of animal or plant that may soon die out

mate   to come together to create young

pregnant   carrying young within the body until the young develop enough to survive outside the mother's body; a female human is pregnant for about nine months; a female elephant is pregnant for 22 months.

prey   an animal hunted for food

teat   the part of the mammary gland that young mammals suck to drink milk

warm-blooded   an animal whose body temperature stays about the same and does not change with the air, ground, or water around it

Index